Marmalade Season

poems

Katie Campbell

first published January 2003 by
IRON Press
5 Marden Tce
Cullercoats
Northumberland
NE30 4PD
England
Tel/fax:: +44 (0)191 253 1901
Email: seaboy@freenetname.co.uk
website: www.ironpress.co.uk

ISBN 0 906228 87 5

printed by
Tyneside Free Press
Charlotte Square
Newcastle upon Tyne

© poems, Katie Campbell
typeset in Georgia 12pt

Cover & Book design by
ironeye design @ IRON Press

Cover painting:
detail from *Still Life with Lemons, Oranges and a Rose, 1633*
Francisco de Zurbarán. Courtesy of The Norton Simon Foundations,
Pasadena, California.

IRON Press Books are available to the trade from
Central Books

Katie Campbell was born in Ottawa in 1957. She got an English degree from McGill University in Montreal and worked on documentaries in New York before moving to London.
As a journalist she has written widely on arts and women's issues, her plays have been performed on stage and radio, and her novel, *The Assumption of the Virgin*, is scheduled for production as a feature film.
She has recently returned to academe to study landscape history. She lives with her husband and daughter, two cats, a tortoise and a macaw.

acknowledgements

Some of the poems in this collection first appeared in the following publications, Canadian and British: Rialto, Critical Quartely, Slow Dancer, Prism International, Poet's Gallery, Descant. 'Aubade' was included in *Paws and Claws*,(Hutchinson, 1995); 'Language for a New Country' was performed as part of the Women's Playhouse Trust's production, *Passages*, Queen Elizabeth Hall, London, 1997.

Other books by Katie Campbell:

What He Really Wants Is A Dog - short stories
Let Us Leave Them Believing - poetry
Live, In The Flesh - fiction
Moon Behind The Clouds: *The Art Of Claude Francis Barry* - biography

poems

9.	Aubade
10.	Trapped
11.	Solo
12.	Decree Absolute
13.	Agape
14.	Memory
15.	Bottoms
16.	Daddy
17.	One O'Clock Club
18.	Random
19.	Jessie On The Beach
20.	More Ancient Than Angels
22.	Fishing
23.	Roses
24.	Water Hole
25.	Mirrors
26.	Going To The Dogs
27.	Madonna Del Parto
28.	Pruning
30.	Through The Glass
31.	Still Life
32.	Hooked
33.	The Craters of The Moon
34.	Caught
35.	This Life
36.	Votive
38.	Waiting
40.	Prelude
42.	Late Night In The West End
44.	A Rose
45.	Landing For a New World
50.	Recipe
51.	Autumn On The St Lawrence
52.	Wilderness
54.	History
55.	Fall
56.	Marmalade Season

*In memory of my mother,
and for Jessica*

Night Feeds

Aubade

I light the candle, fill the tub;
he joins me when he hears the swish
of displaced water.

We talk, at least I talk,
he listens, nods occasionally,
he bats the soap, the sponge, the plug

he likes it when the baby kicks
sending ripples through the surface
from a source that he can't see.

Often when he perches on the edge
his tail dips in the water
like a wick; he doesn't seem to mind-

perhaps he doesn't notice.
Eventually the heat releases both of us,
we sink into a stupor

and sometimes then I think
this is almost enough-
almost a family:

me, the cat, the unborn child.

Trapped

she leaps inside me like a dolphin
lobsided smile wallowing
hippo in a too-tight tub
lugging that lugubrious
weight
      waiting
stretching this bone cage to breaking
pressing her insistent message
against my tightened flesh
resisting that slow twist
into the narrow
inevitable
      passage

Solo

By day the harbour stands, caressed
by the lap and suck of waves,
by night it is revealed to be
a fragile horseshoe curve
which each new tide
erodes.

Suddenly it's my turn to sleep on the outside edge;
curling into a thin half moon
around my newborn babe
who lies, star-fished
across the surface
of this bed

suddenly I wonder
if I really can
contain her.

Decree Absolute

It's something about the company you keep:
your birthmark leaks great pools of sorrow on the sheets
which the silver-tongued snakes drink at night
and the cat steps through, leaving a trail of hieroglyphs.

Suddenly you notice the baby's hands are like a mole's;
she knits them together in an anxious equation
as the milk drip drip drips onto her forehead
slowly she sinks into limbo, into sleep.

So it all comes down to this: a baby crying in the night,
you lying beside her, the cat somewhere
on the edge of the bed scratching to get in,
and the snakes, poised.

Agape

When I think of love now
I think of Jessica,
not of the men behind her.

Suddenly you understand...
a friend said
on the birth of her first child:

the world is not as you thought it was;
language – the word 'love'-
is not the men with whom you make it

but Jessica, curled tight beside you
her forefinger pointed heavenwards
- the pose of Christ Pantocrater

'ruler of everything'-
grunting and snuffling
in her vegetable sleep.

Memory

Each evening I release her
to the bottom of the sea;
she tumbles sometimes like a pebble
or starfishes her limbs:
a sudden memory of depths.

Bottoms

Summer comes and suddenly
all the dragging nappies
are removed

the parks are instantly alive
with gorgeous flocks
of babies' bottoms

fluttering like butterflies
released to their brief glory
in the sun, a thousand tiny moons

luminescent crescents of delight
I'll take a dozen please
a baker's dozen for good luck

bottoms pert – that ghastly word –
plump, pouting, pink
tender tots of lusciousness

delicious bottoms to caress
squeeze, smack, stroke, tease
kiss and tickle, nuzzle, nibble

fragrant bottoms, pungent bottoms
powdered bottoms, primped and patted
such enchantment, firm and fat

and never quite enough, one wants to hoard them -
bottoms which will never be so innocent
again, or so adored.

Daddy

Daddy is home by midnight every night.
These are the things he misses
after kissing us goodbye:

his baby waking at two a.m. screaming
daddymummydaddy
mummydaddy

long slow mornings hammering the postman
into his place in the puzzle, muttering
daddydaddydaddy

the way her face lights up when the wind
rattles the front door and she whispers
daddy?

though she knows daddy doesn't come before dusk
and he's always gone by dawn
like the beast in the fairytale.

ONE O'CLOCK CLUB

It's the shit, you mutter, the endless round
of shit and piss and food: she smears it
throws it, sicks it up – a bit goes through

but the nappies! Where does it come from?!!
You settle her on a pink plastic pig then perch
behind the shield of your paper

taking in stories of women still out there:
the crime-writing, t.v. producer, pianist
who mentions in passing

as she accepts the business award of the year
that she's pregnant again. Breathe deep,
you remind yourself; sometimes you forget to breathe.

You gulp in the fairground smell of grease
from the hamburger van parked at the gate
waiting to ambush health-conscious mothers.

Children whiz round you like random atoms
then four o'clock comes and you're thrown back
onto the carousel of nappies, naps, fish-fingers

and the endless bedtime bubble bath. Finally
as you concede her to sleep and flick out the light
several dinosaurs crunch under foot.

Like the ancients anxious to mask their good fortune
lest the gods get jealous and whisk it away –
you find yourself muttering:
merde merde merde.

Random

I lie, listening to her breathe
waiting for her to wake me with her cries.

The cat comes and goes
unsure of this intrusion in our lives.

How many months has it been,
how many years till I sleep easy again?

It's always the accident
the unforeseen, unanticipated act

the human factor, which creates life/death.
A sudden jarring in the rhythm of her breath:

after all the vitamins and vaccinations
there's still the highway, the IRA

the man with the lollypop beckoning.
Odds are she will survive. Odds are

unreliable. Odds are one in a million
of all the possible combinations

she should be this unique, irreplaceable creature.

Jessie On The Beach

Her tee-shirt is a palette:
raspberry ripple
mustard, coke

her face a pentimento;
tear tracks shine through
the ice-cream smile

she looks up
-a tourist sketch-
runs forward, grins:

a slow-motion picture
stops
caught by a sudden flash

her father's eyes: steel blue
her mother's mouth: bow lips
anxious, a little unsure

sunburnt cheeks and naked
beneath her white cloth hat
bucket and spade in hand

all Victorian postcard
- a seaside scene
or black and white photo

squatting alone in the sand
with the caption 'solitude' or 'happiness'
or 'no message within'.

More Ancient Than Angels

Just here, where her shoulder blades jut out
like willow buds
that's where the wings would sprout.

God takes the ones he loves
Victorians said:
so many angels; so many dead...

She brooks no fig leaves
naked as a flea
bare-assed she capers

peeing where she pleases
no monotheist frowns on this
my nymph - more ancient than angels.

Fishing

Fishing

The Queen will be banished from the bedchamber
if ever the King discovers her secret.
Each evening while he's at work with his papers
she slips through the garden, down to the river
to tease her prey from its fat, wet depths;
her glittering flashes blind their eyes
while she hooks their lips
with her Judas kiss.

They fight and twist but can't resist
as she wrenches them from the warm, brown murk
-where everything's understated and understood –
into the cold, unequivocal blue.
Their eyes white spheres of pulsing fear
they gasp and drown in the crystal air
till she slips her thumb through their chattering teeth.
With one quick snap she breaks them.

ROSES

I keep losing things
-like my perspective, balance
sense of humour, head
over you. My watch has disappeared
my wedding ring too.

Now I'm searching for those twists
to tie my roses to the wall
neat, upright growths
no thorny branches reaching out
to prick unwitting passers by.

I fear my roses thrust their roots
too deep, feeding errant shoots
which spring up
on the wrong side of the fence
and other inappropriate places.

How romantic: roses
strewn across the bedroom floor,
you say. It's simply that I haven't swept in weeks.

The petals drop and dry:
red to pink to brown to grey
to lie amid the dust-
this slow accumulation of debris
which hides the things we've lost.

WATER HOLE

We don't even kiss in greeting anymore
as you would kiss a colleague's wife
or your daughter's best friend's mother.

Occasionally we fuck: rhinoceroses
clanging away in the muddy dregs
after the lions and giraffes and elephants have been

then we rest a moment in the damp
before relinquishing the space
to wart hogs and vultures.

I know you disapprove of extended metaphors
and in this one you'd rather be
among the powerful beasts

the lion, or the dignified giraffe
or have the elephant's sinewy tongue
– but there we are...

The rhino's stub isn't even a horn.
Did you know that? It's matted hair.
Ridiculous really.

Mirrors

Oh that spot on the wall where the mirror was moved;
the rest has dulled, leaving the shape of what was;

even when the party's over and things are back in place
a shadow remains, fading slower than the rest:

the memory of your new *au pair*
dancing with your daughter's father

-not that you were ever so young
or he so old-

but her abandon
and his efforts to connect
and the mirror which you carefully put away

just so it wouldn't break...

Going To The Dogs

Whoever wins gets dinner,
you said; seemed a good bet

I won – I lost: dinner
cost more than my winnings.

Winning with you
I seem to lose.

Madonna del Parto

You part your blue cloak
echoing the flanking angels
holding back the curtains
for the feature show

little do you know –
eyes sunk in that pious smile
your belly thrust, about to split
like some ripe pomegranate

scattering its ruby seed
before the pigeons
scratching in the dirt below-
did I say pigeons? No

I meant the penitents
waiting for their promised King
the sacrifice which you'll deliver up to them
unwittingly

no screams for you: conceived immaculate
-unlike us fallen women
who labour and give birth in pain –
but oh what agonies await you then...

Pruning
(a found-poem on the subject of abortion)

The main reason for pruning
is to keep a plant healthy,
well balanced.

Thin, weak growths are of little use
and should be removed
at first opportunity.

Pruning strengthens plants
preventing diversion
of energy.

Wounds heal quickest
if the cut is clean.

Still Life

Through A Glass
In Memoriam: E.P.C.

A dolphin leapt - a Gothic arc of grace -
framed by the chapel window, while inside
we wept to think of all that death erased.

That final image of your anguished face
-it was as much for you as me, I cried.
A dolphin leapt its Gothic arc of grace

and recklessly it reached up to embrace
the alien air, defying an urgent tide.
We wept to think of all death could erase.

I have returned each summer to that place
to find the dolphin, but the river hides
within its depths its all-consoling grace.

Yet still that moment helped us all to face
your end, your transformation; spirit guide,
the dolphin, left you and your mourners graced.
We wept, but knew then: death does not erase.

Still Life

Sun broadcasts past thick drapes
glances off silver
gleaming oak.

He brings the steaming egg:
places it gently in her cup.
Suddenly her chatter stops.

He bends himself around her,
she waits, he hesitates
that instant of anticipation

before his knife swings to the shell
and makes the crack
that brings the morning flooding back.

Hooked

Six years old: a self-proclaimed vegetarian
strict – no exceptions, not even for bacon –
her rod, several feet taller than she is,
snags branches on the root-tripping trail to the lake.

I row discreetly, slicing a path through the water
whisper sightings, advice;
this is her wish, this expedition,
she's determined to catch her first ever fish.

I've got one! she shrieks, forgetting her vow
of silence. She leaps, almost tipping us
reeling it in like a top; it flips, slashing the water
I pray we can net it before it slips off.
Trapped, neck snapped, it flops in the catch box.

I know that pang of conscience. *Mum,*
she says wanly, *I've had enough.*
I tell her to drag her line. A loon cries.
A moose crashes through the trees.
A beaver splashes into the lake

drawing a quiet line along the horizon.
Night falls fast this far north;
soon we can't see the shore.
Rowing home, suddenly her rod arcs
Another one, she murmurs.

She takes the line and plays it.
It fights, thrashes, churning the darkness beside us.
Not one, but two! Finally they're in, gasping with the rest.
Three fish! she grins. Hooked.

The Craters Of The Moon

A cold, clear night in Hampstead.
Walking friends back to the tube
we pass the observatory – that demi-hemisphere.

On impulse we detour up to the tiny wooden room.
Inside, two lovers drawn by the light, several scientific types
and us... the curious intimacy
of strangers staring at stars.

The telescope pokes accusingly through a revolving roof
magnifying one hundred times
not much against the distance
but enough to show the knife-edge of ash-grey moon
against the black circumference of the universe.

Politely – even Jess hushed –
we take turns to lift an eye to the skies
then relinquish our place to the next in line
because a big cloud is coming.

We push together, slide the roof around
focus in – on Jupiter: two lines of dust,
on Saturn: its rings a stiff tutu of ice,
a halo slipped down to the angel's round belly
in an infant's Christmas play.

A sudden break in the cloud
so we return to the moon:
cratered, like a child has run its finger through a ball of
still-damp clay
leaving pits and trough
... like God's fingerprint on earth.

Caught

Jess, spinning in her crinoline
youngest bridesmaid of all
not easy to keep still
released from the final photo call

goes exploring: ignoring the confetti
she wanders to an ancient cross
caresses its rough edges
its hieroglyphs obscured by moss

then skips off
satin slippers wicking up the dew;
spotting berries among tumbled stones
she flits amid them gobbling flesh, seeds.

Suddenly she's snared.
She struggles, muddy calves bared.
I wince as her apron rips
and hurry to release her

but not before the vigilant photographer
snaps.
Why did you do that! she glares
then strides away

but from that moment on she knows
the camera's waiting.

This Life

I suppose
tucked away in an upstairs room
somebody is always dying.

Those below creep softly,
peeling potatoes, hanging out sheets:
the dull chatter, the subtle averting of conflict.

Suddenly a joke breaks through:
laughter. Silence.
You hurry up the stairs

to soothe the waiting patient
who can still make out the high notes
and the low.

You wipe the forehead, smooth the pillows
change the untouched glass of water.
Finally there is nothing left

you descend again
to wait.

Votive

I wait till the hours compose themselves
into some sort of compatibility
my midnight is her 2 pm - yesterday? tomorrow?

not that it matters. I dial, wondering what to say;
ours is a silent friendship, scanning for seals, beluga
herons stealing our fish

words have never been barriers
but now the generations lie
between us:

Nat, her face like a crumpled paper bag
well into her three score and ten
beer in one hand, fag in the other

rod balancing on boat's bow
while she changes flies
     – all hand-tied...

Suddenly her *Yes?* Cuts through
Nat, it's me. I hear you're not well.
I cringe at such evasion.

*I have cancer. I was writing to tell you.
I didn't want you to find out
from anyone else.*

What sort? I ask,
knowing it's kidney -
quicker than breast, lung, bowel.

I was trekking last month in Nepal
I sent you a tiny yak-bone fish
from the pilgrim's market in Kathmandu.

I'm wearing it this minute
On a thread around my neck, she says.

I smile across the continents
…she's the pilgrim now.

Waiting

At times like this
home becomes neutral space
when Death visits.

Even the piss-smelling cat
is something to care for
- an act that won't be futile.
Death sits by the stair.

You're prepared for it to grab
when you pass up to bed
after pouring one too many.
But it waits.

Next morning it gets you
when, blinded by sun
you wander downstairs
and stub your toe on it, Death;

the floor rises up, you count nails
see dust lodged between boards.
Then, staring out the window
it slips from your mind

as you eye the tangled garden
fantasize the pleasure of cutting back brush:
the rich blood smell of mud
the damp plunge of leaf mould
(the idiotic possibility
of bird song...)

katie campbell

Death makes its move then,
waits in the mouthpiece
as the phone rings.

Prelude

Finally, at forty
she took up piano
simply to learn Bach.

Eschewing love and lovers
she turned on her addiction – passion-
and drove herself

in the mind-aching discipline
of transforming notes
to music:

fingers stretch, brain strains to follow:
algebra, childbirth are nothing
to the agony

like learning to speak
the knowledge is there
the pain is finding the way to it.

Evening after evening
ignoring the dramas being played out
around her, she is mastering her instrument;

the exquisite delight as she no longer hesitates
skittering over the keys, she is becoming
one: brain/hand/hammer

adulteries, betrayals occur
but she sticks to her new tune
the one that goes over and over

the bass repeating like an anchor
the high notes drifting round
variations, expanding, like life, breath

moving, imperceptible, towards the inevitable
but none-the-less, when it comes, surprising
end.

Late Night In The West End

That old cliché: passing a window
you notice a face; not ugly
simply unfamiliar.

You expect the flash of hair
find it faded
even in reflection

you're startled by the eyes:
great bruises, bags
carrying a life.

As you muse
a face stares from the pavement
cut from a four-frame-photo strip

You hesitate to pick it up
-what does it mean?

Already this resembles a scene
in a film: Jarmisch
perhaps Tarrentino.

Suddenly, profoundly tired
you realize the street is empty
and wonder if it is too late

- dangerously late.
Do you owe yourself a cab?
Even now with time creeping away

this concept of owing:
what does one owe oneself
- a self one doesn't even recognize?

A ROSE…

the admen have renamed it middle-youth
to call it middle age would be uncouth
though middle-aged is what we are in truth
only the truly middle aged would be assuaged
by middle-youth.

Language for a New World

i. *Arrival*

Balsam blisters soothe your wounds
it sticks like honey but the relief
it brings is sweet.

Algonquin, Cree

Spruce resin mixed with grease
will patch the leaks
of your canoe.

Ojibawe

For clothing you can chew
the skin of buck and doe
to make it soft enough to sew.

Kanata, Kebec

A ring around the moon means rain.
A mild winter's in store if pelts are thin.
Your routes have all been mapped by the copperskin.

Manhatten, Mississippi

Cedar oil and camphor fight black flies.
For poison oak, witch hazel should suffice.
Suck venom quickly from snake bites.
(The snakes which curl around the rocks and wait

are not so dangerous as the sounds of this new tongue
nor half so fatal if you get them wrong.)

tomahawk, Iroquois, squaw

ii. The Settler Muses

Ice retreats.
Earth shows through in patches;
soon it will be soft enough
to break.

Spring skies small and mean
reflect the yellow eyes
of hungry beasts

creeping in the undergrowth.
Shadows - those savages -
who stare, steal

curse us till the Black Robes
buy their souls with trinkets
trifles

but worse are the English
their dreams of dominion
their rifles.

iii. The Mohawk Observes Her Neighbour

He brings fire water
and the spotted disease
which decimate our people
faster than the angry gods
of famine and drought.

Our spirit beings
displease his chief
who rules our people too, he says;
the dead man hung on crossed poles
will save our souls.

For what? I say
if deer are slaughtered
and forests burned
for row on row
of dull potatoes.

Where will our souls reside
and who will feed them?
The flesh of this one man will not go far I fear
... and what then?

iv. Last Words

In the chapel where she's laid
it reads: 'a little half-breed maid'.

The family Bible is inscribed:
'John, an Indian boy
possession of Alex Roy, Esquire
baptised, twelfth May'.

Autumn on the St Lawrence

The Recipe

Making the marmalade without you;
last year it was a ritual of mourning
this year it's a tribute: squeezing pith
picking out pips, slicing the skin fine.

It's the first year I haven't drawn blood
the first time I haven't needed that stained page
in your spidery writing –
I seem to know it by heart.

I never told you this, but once I tried to make it
from a magazine – none of your endless waiting:
stand twelve hours, boil, stand one day...
The marmalade was tasteless.

Today my daughter humours me;
she licks the spoon,
wondering why we don't buy it from the shop
like everyone else.

Those small jars you filled with such care
- for years I wished you'd swap them for a job.
Now I understand it: homemade marmalade is rare.

Autumn On The St. Lawrence

The trees are turning, you note
as you always do
these last afternoons

counting off the days
the end of the holiday
another summer sloughed.

Deciduous tips poke pink
through the screen of pine
the mountains behind.

You will leave here for another year
with relief, regret.
Rain ripens the berries,

autumn's compensation,
rainbows arc the river
framing whales that sing

deep, where you can't see them
– still you scan the water
for one more look.

Wilderness

The fire snaps, hisses.
The baby sighs
in her sleep.

You pull out the log book,
yesterday's catch:
two rods, three hours

twenty-four fish.
Rain on the roof.
The baby moans

re-living the journey:
five miles in the back of a truck
heat like an oven

the baby sweating
turning grey
wilting.

Wild strawberries dotted the trail
like drops of blood
Now fishes' eyes

shimmer -
the glee of the fishermen
counting their catch.

You try to join in their triumph
but you can't shake the image:
your baby, the ovens.

This annual pilgrimage into the wild:
we carry our wilderness with us.

History

It happened: we were swinging along
singing a sort of a song for the baby
nothing sustained, nothing with any heart in it really

the *fraises des bois* were already over
the raspberries not yet ripe
when there, up ahead, as we ambled along...

– each of the thirty-five years of my life
I've trod this path and never seen one
... spore, yes, purple splashing the forest floor

moose I've seen, and beaver
coon, even poachers lurking in the cedary coves
but never before...

it stared

we drew up slowly into a group
it eyed us a full thirty seconds
then lumbered away

slowly we moved on
keeping together now
even the baby subdued

sun darting through birch leaves
butterflies flicking the air
– and the bear.

Fall

I smelled it this morning
the first chill – a shiver
quickly burned off by the sun
but the impulse was triggered –
that mothball scent of loss.

The time has come when as guests go
we don't remake their beds;
sheets are slipped into the linen press
blankets folded into trunks and one by one
the doors along the corridor are closed.

Although the afternoon's still warm
children come in early from their games.
Old friends pick their way along the path
to say good-bye. Geese begin to gather.

Suddenly you notice gold flicker
in the woods, trees edged red –
it happens
        all of a sudden
the night sky, like a pierced-tin lantern
flashes with falling stars.

Marmalade Season

It's five years yesterday since you died
and marmalade season again

each year it gets easier
fleshy slices slip from the knife

the time it takes to keep them thin
is not so precious now

your apple tree is still alive
it seemed to fade, then suddenly this summer

it was full of tight, white buds
they never ripened

but blossoms are enough
anyway I'm told the fruit is bitter

like these Seville oranges
before they are distilled

I'm learning to simmer them slowly, stirring
stirring, to get the clear, gold hue

these small acts of concentration
a slow preparation…